Romance is God's Idea

10 Steps to Add
More Sizzle to Your Marriage

Sabrina McDonald

CHISELBOOKS

Romance is God's Idea: 10 Steps to Add More Sizzle to Your Marriage
Copyright © 2024 by Sabrina McDonald. All rights reserved.

No part of this publication may be reproduced, stored in a retrieval system, or transmitted in any way by any means—electronic, mechanical, photocopy, recording or otherwise—without prior permission of the copyright holder, except as provided by USA copyright law.

The author of this publication is responsible for all editing and proofreading and responsible for any errors in the finished product.

Unless otherwise stated, scripture references are taken from the English Standard Version Bible, © 2001 by Crossway Bibles, a publishing ministry of Good News Publishers.

Details in some anecdotes and stories have been changed to protect the identities of the persons involved.

Published in the United States of America.

For my mom, Willena Joyce

Contents

Introduction: Romance is God's Idea

Step 1: Define romance.

Step 2: Know your spouse.

Step 3: Give up the soul mate fantasy.

Step 4: Don't maintain impossible standards.

Step 5: Put your mind in the mood.

Step 6: Purify your marriage.

Step 7: Pull the weeds of bitterness.

Step 8: Pay attention.

Step 9: Grow together spiritually.

Step 10: Don't threaten to leave.

Conclusion: God is the Great Romancer

Bonus: Ideas for a More Romantic Bedroom

Introduction:
Romance is God's Idea

I was working on romance content for a marriage ministry when one of the editors stopped and wondered out loud, "Is the idea of *romance* even biblical?"

That's a good question. I think most Christians would agree *marriage* is biblical. After all, God created Adam and Eve, male and female, at the beginning of time. He blessed them and told them to multiply (Genesis 1:27-28).

Throughout scripture marriage is often used as a symbol of God's love for his people. The church is often referred to as the "bride" and Christ as our "bridegroom." Jesus tells parables using this imagery, and the apostle Paul emphasizes the symbolism of marriage, explaining it as a metaphor for the Gospel: Husbands lay down your lives as Christ died for the church, and wives submit to your husbands as the church submits to Christ (Ephesians 5:22-33).

But anyone who's married knows *romance* is not the same as *marriage*. Romance isn't even the same as *sex*. So, what is romance? And how do we know it pleases God?

That's what we're going to explore in the next few chapters. And we'll delve into some practical tips on how to get the sizzle back into your relationship. I hope you'll soon discover, not only is romance beautiful and wonderful, it's also God's idea.

Romance is God's Idea

Step 1:
Define Romance

How do You Define Romance?

When I married Robbie his favorite time to introduce "romance" was in the middle of a fight. I think he thought his gestures would stop the fumes coming out my ears. It didn't work.

Years later, we still disagree on our ideas of romance. I often remind him that sitting together on the couch with the television blaring, while he surfs social media and I piddle with my hobbies, does not add up to "spending time together." He can't understand why that many hours in the same vicinity doesn't count for something.

Recently, a man named Don said he had the same problem. His wife, too, was disappointed, that they weren't "spending time together." But Don was perplexed. Since he and his wife both started working from home, he was spending more time with her than ever before. He thought that was sufficient, but when he left to go hunting or fishing with friends, she was hurt.

Both Don and my husband have come to their wit's end, trying to figure out how to make us wives happy, and they' re not alone.

After talking with other exasperated couples, I'm convinced romance has acquired a case of mistaken identity. Neither husband nor wife can define what romance is, but they do know when they haven't had it.

It's especially frustrating when there's been a lot of talking, but nothing seems to change. Truth is, you can talk about fixing your romance problem all day, but unless you and your spouse are working with the same definition, there's no real understanding.

So, let's find out. How does one define "romance"?

What Romance is Not

Before we get into what romance is, let's first establish what romance is *not*.

Romance is not love. Love is far more important. Love is a commitment, a spiritual bond, a promise kept. For anyone thinking, "My spouse must not love me because he/she is never romantic," stop right there.

It's not "romantic" to bring home a paycheck or raise children. It's not romantic to take care of a sick spouse or stay married when times are hard. But all of that is *loving*—the deepest kind of love. Romance can be created by anyone at any time. But real love can only be achieved by determination and hard work.

Romance is not sex. Sex *can* be romantic. The ancient writer said, "Three things are too wonderful for me, four that I can't figure out: the way of an eagle in the sky, the way of a snake on the rock, the way of a ship out on the open sea, and the way of a man with a young woman" (Proverbs 30:18-19 CSB).

There is beauty in appreciating your spouse's body, looking into one another's eyes, and whispering sweet nothings. The closeness and connection that sex creates is supernatural within God's holy bounds.

But sex can also be very *un*romantic—selfish, one-sided, and cold. When one spouse turns sex into an emotionless goal of self-pleasure, it becomes a romance killer. Many women treated this way only participate in sex out of obligation or as a bargaining tool. It becomes ugly, dark, and not romantic in the least.

What Romance Is

So, what is romance, then? Romance is simply an act of wooing someone. Remember the days before marriage when you planned ahead to send flowers, go on dinner dates, and sometimes dancing or a picnic? Those weren't expressions of *love*—you can't love someone you barely know. Those were signals. You were trying to draw this person to you.

You wanted this person to know they were worth spending money on and sacrificing time and resources. You wanted them to see the best in you, too, by dressing and presenting well. You wanted that person to be impressed.

So now that you've won, what's the point of romance? I'm glad you asked!

Romance in marriage says, "You're still important to me." Your spouse wants to know you still appreciate and value him/her. Romance shows you still have a willingness to sacrifice time and money. That's why flowers and dinner dates matter—you want your spouse to know your relationship is still a priority to you.

Romance says, "I know you." Everyone wants to know and be known. God made us that way. Your wife doesn't just want flowers. She wants to know you're thinking of her. Your husband doesn't just want sex. He wants to know you still find him attractive and enjoy being close to him.

Romance keeps the marriage motors running. Dennis Rainey, author of *Staying Close: Stopping the Natural Drift Toward Isolation in Marriage*, once said marriage is like two boats in the ocean. If you don't keep the motors running, the boats naturally drift apart.

In the same way, if you don't work to stay close emotionally, one day when your children are grown and gone, you and your spouse will wake up as strangers. Romance maintains and strengthens the bond between you so it lasts even after the kids leave the nest.

Love Quotes

All his faults are such that one loves him still the better for them.
-Oliver Goldsmith
The Good-Natur'd Man [1768]

The supreme happiness of life is the conviction that we are loved.
-Victor Hugo
Les Misérables [1862]

Thou art the book, the library whereon I look.
-Henry King
"The Exequy" [1657]

Romance is God's Idea

Step 2:
Know Your Spouse

Know Your Spouse

Now that you have a working definition, what should romance look like in your relationship? That depends on your spouse's personality and preferences. Romance is different for everyone. A girlfriend of mine hates to receive flowers. She thinks they're a waste of money and would rather go horseback riding. Another friend wants her husband to clean the kitchen while she takes a bath.

I told Don his wife wanted to spend time with him but not sitting around the house, and it didn't have to be "girly" fun. One of the best trips Robbie and I took was a guided fishing trip. I've never seen him more in love with me than when I pulled a three-pound brown trout into the boat. The trick is to know your spouse.

Men, 1 Peter 3:7 says, "Husbands, live with your wives in an understanding way." Know her favorite flowers and colors. Pay attention to what makes her happy.

Women, Ephesians 5:33 says, "Let the wife see that she respects her husband." Appreciate his hobbies and interests. Let him teach you about the things he loves, and use that knowledge to show how much you appreciate him.

You might have heard of the Five Love Languages, based on the book by Gary Chapman. Ask your spouse (don't guess) which love language speaks romance to her/him, and then fill up their love tank with the way *they* speak romance.

It takes work, sacrifice, and time, but your attempts at romance are worth it. They may not be perfect, but anything you do to make your spouse feel known sows seeds of love that will bear fruit your whole life long.

The Five Love Languages

Author and marriage counselor Gary Chapman discovered five basic ways people express and receive love. Most people recognize their primary and secondary love languages right away, but you can also take the free quiz at 5lovelanguages.com.

Acts of Service
These people feel loved when something is done for them, instead of receiving a gift, hug, or compliment.

Receiving Gifts
These people feel loved when they receive a thoughtful gift. It can be small or large because it's the thought that counts.

Quality Time
These people want to spend time with the people they love. They enjoy making memories. The key is "quality," not time.

Words of Affirmation
These people love to hear a sincere compliment. They want to hear others express pride, admiration, and affirmation. It can be spoken or written.

Physical Touch
These people feel loved when they are touched in a loving way. This isn't always sex. It can also be things like holding hands, cuddling, or back rubs.

Find out more at 5lovelanguages.com.

Romance is God's Idea

Step 3: Give up the Soul Mate Fantasy

Give up the Soul Mate Fantasy

The Hallmark fairytale of finding your one true "soul mate" has ruined the happiness of too many marriages to count. I personally know many who have fallen prey to this deceiving fantasy.

I knew a young lady who divorced her husband after the first year of marriage because she was convinced he wasn't her "soul mate." She figured their differences meant there was something wrong with their relationship. It was clear to her, he wasn't tailor made for all her hopes and desires.

Another girl I talked to had been married to her high school sweetheart for nearly two decades. She started to wonder if she missed her one true "soul mate" because she got married so young. Thankfully, through Bible study and encouragement, she realized her husband was the only soul mate she needed.

Most people think your soul mate is someone who never upsets or disappoints you and only inspires beautiful moments of laughter in the sunset for the rest of your lives.

If you're questioning whether you married your soul mate, stop wondering. As long as your spouse isn't abusive or adulterous, then your spouse is all the soul mate you need.

The truth is a soul mate isn't someone you *find*, it's someone you intentionally and prayerfully *become*. A happy marriage doesn't automatically happen when you find the "right" person. It comes by two people working hard to maintain the love they share.

Nowhere in the Bible does God say anything about

finding a soul mate. It does say, however, "the two shall become one flesh" (Genesis 2:24). This doesn't mean husband and wife grow together physically like trees, but that their blood is mingled and their souls are intertwined.

When two people love God and work hard to know each other, serve each other's needs, and find ways to express their love, they wake up one day and realize the soul mate they always wanted is right by their side.

Quotes on Companionship

"There is no more lovely, friendly, and charming relationship, communion, or company than a good marriage."
-Martin Luther

One must learn love and go through a good deal of suffering to get to it ... and the journey is always towards the other soul.
-D. H. Lawrence

A friend is one to whom one may pour out all the contents of one's heart ... knowing that gentle hands will take and sift it, [and] keep what is worth keeping.
-George Eliot

Romance is God's Idea

Step 4: Don't Maintain Impossible Standards

Don't Maintain Impossible Standards

Hollywood and culture have done marriages a terrible disservice, not only with the soul mate fantasy, but also by creating impossible standards for love and romance.

Let's face it—most of married life is boring. We spend much of our time discussing problems, watching TV, and working on household chores. It's not always roses and romantic music. Most husbands aren't going to be Carey Grant, and most wives aren't going to be Marilyn Monroe. And that's okay!

Instead of comparing your spouse to your favorite movie heartthrob, why not appreciate all the wonderful attributes of the person you're married to. And when he/she attempts to do something romantic, it might not be as good as a Hollywood movie set, but with a change in perspective, maybe you can appreciate the authenticity.

Think of it—in the movies, settings are hand-selected; costumes are custom designed; actors and actresses are put on diets and filmed at the most flattering angles. Your spouse can't possibly compete with imaginary people and settings.

I'm sure your local Olive Garden doesn't compare to the New York City bar and grill in your favorite romcom, but it may be all your spouse can afford. Why not be thankful for a partner that doesn't go into debt just to reach an impossible standard?

Or maybe you keep comparing your spouse to a person in real life, not Hollywood. Maybe it's a friend's spouse, perhaps, or a co-worker. You look at another person's marriage and wonder why your own isn't as wonderful as theirs.

Maybe your friend's wife always seems to look her best, but your wife doesn't seem to try anymore. Maybe your co-worker's husband always remembers birthdays and anniversaries, but your husband forgets every year.

Remember, you can't see the whole picture. You're only seeing part of their story. Many people put on a lovely mask in public, especially on social media. But under the surface, they have as many problems and weaknesses as any marriage.

Whenever you feel tempted to think, "My friend's wife would never look like that," or "My co-worker's husband would never forget," stop and thank God for something good about your own spouse.

This small change in perspective is sometimes all it takes to improve your attitude, and it's what grace in marriage looks like. It gives your spouse permission to fall short of perfection while still receiving all your love.

If you're having trouble understanding why you should love someone when they haven't "earned" it, remember God offers the same kind of grace to all of us. We don't deserve his love. We continue to fail the standard of perfection. And yet he blesses us anyway.

Grace in marriage is beautiful—it's like a lovely waltz of give and take, leading and following, falling and helping the other get up again. Grace never gives up on the potential for happiness together.

But grace is only possible if you put down the score card. Keep loving your spouse, no matter how often you're disappointed, and eventually the seeds of grace sown in your marriage will produce the fruit of lasting happiness.

Romance is God's Idea

Step 5: Put Your Mind in the Mood

Put Your Mind in the Mood

Having romance in your marriage is as much about the mind as it is the body. That's because the mind and body are inseparable. A person's thoughts control the body's reactions. For example, if you think about food, your mouth begins to salivate. If you watch a scary movie, your heart may begin to race.

The sex drive is no different. How you think about your spouse will determine how much you enjoy being intimate with him/her. Put your mind in the mood and your body will follow.

Now, wait a minute. You may be thinking, "I thought you said romance *wasn't* sex?" Actually, I said sex *may* or *may not* be romantic. But sex is important in marriage for many reasons. It creates a bond. It also protects husbands and wives against temptation and sexual immorality (1 Corinthians 7:2-5).

Since sex is an essential part of marriage, it's important to make sure it's romantic and enjoyable for both partners.

One way to do that is by putting your mind in the mood. Most of us have many distractions and worries—aging parents, bosses and co-workers, problems with children. And sometimes thoughts about a spouse are the last priority. But that's exactly why it's important to focus on him/her.

Practice loving and admiring thoughts about your spouse throughout the day. Philippians 4:8 says, "Finally, brethren, whatever is true, whatever is honorable, whatever is right, whatever is pure, whatever is lovely, whatever is of good repute, if there is any excellence and if anything worthy of praise, dwell on these things."

What do you still find attractive—eyes, arms, smile, kind heart, funny jokes, tender embrace? Take a minute during the day to picture those things.

Also include fun memories. Think back when you and your spouse were most in love. Maybe it was when you first met, or the early years of your marriage. Let the happiness of those memories sink into your heart.

Even if you've completely lost that "lovin' feelin'" you can think of *something* good about your spouse. Start at any point. And then express that admiration verbally or through text. You might make a sweet social media post expressing your appreciation for your spouse. (Keep it family friendly!) The more you concentrate on the good, the more your heart will soften.

Then, in the evening before bed, think about making love to your spouse. If it would help you feel sexy, take a shower or wear some cologne. Put on sexy pajamas.

During intimacy, enjoy the moment. Don't let your mind wander to your schedule tomorrow or worries of life. Try to ignore distractions. Relax your body—that alone can make the process more pleasurable, especially for women.

For more tips on how to make love in a pleasurable way, refer to the book *Sexual Intimacy in Marriage* by William Cutrer, M.D., and Sandra Glahn. It's a very appropriate and practical book on sexuality for married couples from both medical and biblical perspectives.

The mind is the most powerful love-making tool in your relationship. And that's why the next step discusses the importance of purifying the thought life.

Romance is God's Idea

Step 6:
Purify Your Marriage

Purify Your Marriage

Sex inside of marriage is a beautiful expression of love. God ordained the intimacy between man and wife in scripture: "The man and his wife were both naked and were not ashamed" (Genesis 2:25).

The nakedness is a symbol of a married couple's innocence. It means there are no secrets or shame between you. You are one with your spouse, "bone of my bones and flesh of my flesh" (Genesis 2:23). Sex was made to be a special gift that you share only with this one person until one of you dies.

I hope it's obvious that involving any other people in lovemaking is a sin. That includes affairs, swinging, threesomes, and any other sexual activity, even among consenting adults. But what's less understood and more common are sexual sins of the mind, like pornography, lust, and erotic movies and literature.

Some couples use porn and other forms of erotica as foreplay. That's a bad idea for a couple of reasons.

First, over time porn loses its arousing effect, so in order to accomplish the same level of excitement, content must get raunchier and more perverse. That can ultimately lead to unspeakably debased content and even illegal activity, with some people acting out their fantasies in real life.

Second, when making love, you should be giving all of you—body, mind, and soul—to your spouse, not just body.

I once heard a woman tell a friend if she's having trouble in the bedroom, she should imagine the face of a sexy actor on her husband's head. That may seem like a harmless prop, but consider, when you're in the middle of lovemaking, do you want your spouse to be thinking about you or an erotic porn star?

Jesus took our thought life very seriously. He said, "...Everyone who looks at a [person] with lust ... has already committed adultery [of the] heart" (Matthew 5:28).

Erotic images and literature hurt marriages in many ways. As we talked about before, erotica sets up unrealistic expectations for your spouse. Porn stars have bodies that are surgically altered, making normal bodies look subpar.

Real people can't compete with the stamina and performance of actors and actresses who are paid to look like they enjoy the experience, even when some scenes are clearly abusive.

A regular diet of erotica can become an addiction. Watching or reading about sex becomes more important than real intimacy with your spouse. Some people even have a "favorite" porn actor and begin replacing thoughts of their spouse with a fantasy.

That kind of betrayal hurts a marriage partner, who feels overlooked, unloved, and disappointed. The hurt spouse may become jealous and distrustful. Even if the "other person" is just on a screen, it has the same effect as a real physical affair.

Excessive erotica and porn consumption can also cause medical problems, like impotency, erectile dysfunction, or the inability to achieve sexual satisfaction with your spouse.

All of this is dire information, especially if you're already addicted to porn or erotica. But it's not too late. If you remove the stimulant of pornography, your brain can heal and eventually function normally without it.

The damage done to the relationship with your spouse can also heal. When you cleanse lust from your marriage, the bond with your spouse becomes stronger in every way—sexually, mentally, and spiritually.

And it's possible for your relationship to regain healthy characteristics that may have been lost, such as, trust, friendship, and appreciation.

Impurity in your life will bring about suffering. But when you honor God and remove the sin, your life will reap the benefits of his blessings, inside and outside the marriage bed.

Confession and Repentance:

1. Evaluate your relationship with your spouse. Is there something you need to ask forgiveness for? Is there something you need to extend forgiveness for that you've bitterly held onto?

2. Get on your knees in front of your spouse tonight, and confess, repent, forgive, and receive forgiveness.

3. This week memorize 1 John 1:9: "If we confess our sins, he is faithful and just to forgive us our sins and to cleanse us from all unrighteousness."

Romance is God's Idea

Step 7: Pull the Weeds of Bitterness

Pull the Weeds of Bitterness

I hope by now you realize the important role of your thought life when it comes to romance in your marriage. The way you think about your spouse controls the amount and quality of your affection. Good thoughts are key to romance in marriage.

But to make room for good thoughts, that also mean you have to reduce the number of negative thoughts. An overly critical attitude and tendency toward fault-finding will only make your spouse withdraw emotionally, which is a romance killer.

Because married couples' lives are so intricately intertwined, it's easy to see a spouse's problems and mistakes. We forget sometimes everyone has flaws, and sadly, we can be the harshest critic of those we love most.

But if you want a romantic marriage and healthy love life, it's important to train the mind to overlook petty annoyances and concentrate on the good.

The Apostle Paul encourages Christians to "take every thought captive to the obedience of Christ" (2 Corinthians 10:5). When you hear your mind starting to rant about your spouse's inconsiderate habits and hurtful mistakes, train yourself to stop and consider if these "problems" are really all that bad.

Marriage has to be a place where forgiveness reigns supreme. Unforgiven transgressions will create bitterness in your heart. And bitterness grows like a weed in the garden of your love—it chokes out all the fruit and flowers and eventually kills your relationship.

Hebrews 12:14-15 says, "Strive for peace with

everyone, and for the holiness without which no one will see the Lord. See to it that no one fails to obtain the grace of God; that no 'root of bitterness' springs up and causes trouble, and by it many become defiled." Unforgiveness in your marriage often causes more pain than the original transgression.

When conflicts arise, it's easy to find fault in a spouse and hard to see how we played a role in the problem. If you find yourself pointing the finger most of the time, remember to take the log out of your own eye before taking the speck out of your spouse's eye (Matthew 7:5). Usually there is blame to be taken on both sides.

If you find it hard to feel romantic toward your spouse, check for bitterness or unforgiveness in your heart. Consider how you can gently confront the problem, work to find common ground, and reconcile. This small step can be the catalyst that brings healing to your marriage and opens the door for closer connection.

> Stive for peace with everyone, and for the holiness without which no one will see the Lord. See to it that no one fails to obtain the grace of God; that no "root of bitterness" springs up and causes trouble, and by it many become defiled.
>
> **Hebrews 12:14-15**

Romance is God's Idea

Step 8:
Pay Attention

Pay Attention

Rekindling romance in your relationship is a lot easier when you act in ways that make your spouse feel loved, but there's not a universal checklist. Like I said before, each person's idea of romance depends on personality, taste, and preferences.

So how do you know what makes your spouse feel loved? It's simple and difficult at the same time: You pay attention and study your spouse.

Sometimes that means simply asking. My husband and I sometimes ask each other, "How is your love tank?" And by that, we mean, "Am I doing enough to make you feel loved?"

If one of us says our love tank is "low," then the other spouse knows it's time for a special date night, weekend getaway, or some other treat.

But sometimes paying attention to your spouse is less direct and requires looking for clues. You might notice your spouse browsing a retail store or internet shop. Listen to what he/she mentions and take note. You might even keep a list of your spouse's preferences, needs, and gift ideas.

This might sound obvious, but it's also important to remember special dates—wedding anniversaries, Valentine's Day, birthdays. If this is hard for you, put reminders on your computer or phone calendar.

You can also plan ordinary days to celebrate your relationship, just because. It doesn't have to be elaborate. Send flowers for no reason. Email a love letter, or text messages with emojis. Write on dozens of sticky notes and hide them around the house. Do something that says, "Surprise! I still love you as much as I always have."

Another overlooked key to romance is a beautiful bedroom. People often put their nicest decorations in rooms where guests will mingle and put the lesser décor in the bedroom. We also tend to hide messes like unfolded laundry or stacks of paperwork in the bedroom, as well.

But the bedroom should be one of the most important rooms in the house because it's a sanctuary for your relationship, and a healthy relationship is the foundation of the home.

Decorate and maintain the bedroom to create an atmosphere where you enjoy spending time. (See the bonus section at the end of the book for tips on how to have a more romantic bedroom.)

No matter how you speak romance, what's most important is that you pay attention to your spouse and find out what best speaks romance to him/her.

It can be intimidating to come up with ideas, but remember, your attempts don't have to be perfect. Your spouse will know you tried, and sometimes just trying to be romantic is the most romantic thing you can do in a marriage.

Romantic Ideas

Hide love notes around the house.

Plan a picnic.

Go fishing together.

Write a love letter or a song.

Play board games.

Send flowers.

Wrap a small gift.

Go bowling.

Take your spouse to his/her favorite restaurant.

Go out for ice cream.

Spread flower petals on the bed.

Light candles.

Complete a chore your spouse wants finished.

Watch a romantic movie.

Make a list of your spouse's best qualities.

Send a thoughtful text message.

Give your spouse a foot or back rub.

Turn off your phone.

Go for a walk.

Dance in the living room to your favorite song.

Romance is God's Idea

Step 9:
Grow Together Spiritually

Grow Together Spiritually

When people think of romance, Bible study and prayer usually aren't the first images that come to mind. Yet growing together spiritually is one of the best investments for romance you can make.

Many spouses have regular sexual activity, but they don't achieve true *intimacy*—they miss out on the soul, the person underneath the flesh.

Solomon said, "a threefold cord is not quickly broken" (Ecclesiastes 4:12). In a marriage, that third cord is Christ. He's the bond that makes a marriage strong and sturdy, so when he isn't the center, everything else falls apart.

Growing together spiritually starts with being part of a church family. It doesn't have to be a large church, maybe just a group that meets in a home. The size doesn't matter, but what does matter is regular attendance.

That way when there are troubles in your marriage (and they always come), you have godly friends, teachers, and pastors to help you stay strong through the challenges and offer counsel from God's word.

Aim to pray together regularly, work Bible studies together, and share with each other the things God is teaching you. By sharing your spiritual journey, you'll both keep walking in the same direction toward God.

Scripture is also full of advice for married couples. You'll find practical guidelines and instructions for both husbands and wives. And you'll also find stories of couples in the Bible who will challenge and inspire you.

The Song of Solomon is a steamy romance book all about the love between a man and his bride. And there are others like Ruth and Boaz or Hosea and Gomer that show us how a loving relationship can prevail. There is no shortage of verses that can help you have a strong beautiful marriage.

I also want to encourage you to pray for your spouse. This is one way to keep bitterness from creeping into your heart. It's hard to hold grudges against someone when you're praying God's blessings and protection over his/her life.

But more than that, God answers our prayers. If your spouse is struggling, who better to pray than you? Your whole family will benefit from your prayers, as well as, your growing relationship.

Romance is a lot easier when you know and understand someone from the inside out. The more you cultivate your marriage on a spiritual level, the deeper your relationship roots will grow, making the outward expression of your love healthy and strong.

Of course, this kind of spiritual growth can only happen for spouses who have made Jesus Christ their Lord and Savior through the power of the Holy Spirit. If you're not a Christian, or you're not sure, find out more at *billygraham.org/story/how-to-be-born-again/*.

Prayer Guide for Your Spouse

Monday: Pray for your spouse's relationship with Christ. Ask the Holy Spirit to build a fire in his/her heart that burns with passion.

Tuesday: Ask God to put godly influences in your spouse's life at work, church, and in the community.

Wednesday: Pray for a heart of compassion that wants to influence the world for Christ. Whether through local organizations or personal ministry, pray for a heart that reaches out.

Thursday: Our world has no shortage of indulgences, and Satan is prowling. Pray your spouse will be protected from temptation.

Friday: Pray your spouse will have courage in difficult circumstances, to stand for truth, and do the right thing, no matter the cost.

Saturday: Christianity is not a dead boring religion. It should be full of celebration. Pray your spouse will live an abundant life full of grace.

Sunday: Pray for rest in mind and body. Too much stress takes away the joys in life and distracts the spirit.

Romance is God's Idea

Step 10:
Never Threaten to Leave

Never Threaten to Leave

The final step on how to add romance to your marriage is to remove the threat of divorce. This sounds like a simple concept, yet many people make the mistake of threatening to leave early in the relationship, causing catastrophic damage. Those words plant seeds of fear and mistrust and can take months or years to heal.

Spouses are going to get into arguments. That's a given. And healthy disagreements are good because they're usually a sign of honest communication.

The problem comes when one spouse invokes the d-word (divorce) in the middle of a yelling match. Most people don't mean it seriously when they spout off in the heat of anger, but words hurt, and they can't be taken back.

Marriage is a covenant which means it's a promise that is meant to last until death (Matthew 19:3-9). Obviously, there are a few reasons to end a marriage, but that decision should never be taken lightly. Non-serious issues like financial woes or feeling disconnected, sadly, are most often cited as the cause of divorce.

Although there may need to be changes in your marriage and even counseling, resist the temptation to threaten divorce because of disagreements. Allowing divorce to remain an option weakens your resolve to work out your problems.

Instead, act as if divorce is not an option and determine to work through any issues you have. Tell your spouse you will honor your vows and never leave. Let your spouse know you plan to keep your promise for a lifetime.

By removing the threat of divorce, you build trust in your marriage. Your spouse feels safe and assured that you are both in the relationship for the long haul.

That gives a spouse the courage to invest in the relationship wholistically—body, mind, and soul.

It's hard to devote your life and love to your spouse when there's always the question in the back of your mind whether your efforts will be in vain.

Most marital problems can be resolved if both spouses are determined to do so. And the best part is making up! Lots of romance can happen when tempers are cooled and compromise has been made.

With each reconciliation, your marriage bond grows stronger, and your spouse is reassured once again that your marriage will make it for a lifetime.

> "So they are no longer two but one flesh. What therefore God has joined together, let not man separate."
>
> -Jesus (Matthew 19:6)

Romance is God's Idea

Conclusion: God is the Great Romancer

God is the Great Romancer

I hope you can see by now that romance is God's idea. But he doesn't just *tell* us how to have a romantic relationship, he also *shows* us by his own love.

God longs to be with his people, but he doesn't hit us over the head and drag us off like some cave man. He woos us and calls us gently and patiently. Before we ever knew him, the Holy Spirit reached out with his irresistible presence to draw us in.

Jesus said, "No one can come to me unless the Father who sent me draws him" (John 6:44). It's God's calling that initiates our relationship with him, not the other way around.

The book of Hosea illustrates this perfectly. The story of Hosea and Gomer is an allegory representing God and his people.

It's about a man who marries a harlot. He treats her with kindness and is a good husband to her. Yet she is determined not to love him and goes back to her corrupt life and lovers. But Hosea will not give up, bringing her home time and again.

In the same way, God loves us, gives us blessings, and yet we continually turn away from him. But God is determined to win our love. As Hosea said, "Therefore, behold, I will allure her, bring her into the wilderness, and speak kindly to her" (Hosea 2:14).

Even though we don't deserve the gracious and abundant love of God, he gives it freely anyway.

The Bible is full of romantic stories like this one. The Song of Solomon is an entire book dedicated to a man admiring the love of his bride.

In another book, Jacob loved Rachel so much he worked 14 years to get permission to marry her.

Another story is about Boaz, a rich man who loved a poor widow from a foreign land. Not only did he give her a new life, he also took care of her mother-in-law.

You see, God is a hopeless (or should I say hopeful) romantic, is he not?

There's a reason why God so often uses imagery of bride and groom to illustrate his love for his people. This isn't some worn out boring love. He delights in us like a newlywed. As Isaiah 62:5 says, "And as the bridegroom rejoices over the bride, so your God will rejoice over you."

God's love for us isn't begrudging, reluctant, or out of pity. His love is exuberant! As Solomon's bride exclaimed, "His banner over me [is] love" (Song of Solomon 2:4). God raises a flag over our heads, waving it high for all the world to see, exclaiming, "My beloved is mine" (Song of Solomon 6:3).

Jesus loved us so much, he even sacrificed his own life so we could be together for all eternity. It doesn't get any more romantic than that.

Yes, God is a romantic. And as his people, it's our job to reflect the same kind of pursuing, exuberate, sacrificial love in our marriages.

Sometimes it's hard, but it's always worth it. Aren't you glad God never grows tired of romancing us? And may we never grow tired of showing that same kind of love to our spouses.

Romance is God's Idea

Bonus: Ideas for a More Romantic Bedroom

Bonus: Ideas for a More Romantic Bedroom

Marriage is the most intimate relationship two people on earth can have. As Genesis 2:25 describes Adam and Eve, husbands and wives are "naked and not ashamed." Yet the one place where marital fidelity is most intimate—the bedroom—is often treated as a storeroom for clutter.

Instead, the bedroom should be a place where love and romance are cultivated, encouraged, and celebrated. This is the one room where you and your spouse can enjoy the relationship God created for you to share, so there should be special attention paid to it.

Women are especially affected by the state of the bedroom because we feel connected to the home in a personal way. We often see the home as an extension of our personalities and style. The colors, wall decorations, furniture, pictures, etc., are all selected based on what we want others to know about us.

Ask yourself this question: If a friend were to walk into your bedroom today, what would she say about your marriage based on what she found? If the answer to that question leaves you feeling inadequate, these 10 ideas will help you turn your bedroom into an incubator for romance.

1. Put away clutter. Everyone has them—stacks of bills, coupons, random newsletters that haven't been read. And since you don't want to forget about them, the default system is to make a stack on the dresser in your bedroom.

Perhaps the dirty laundry has found a gathering place

on the floor next to the bed. And all those children's paintings you held on to, are stacked around the mirror.

If you want a romantic bedroom, all this clutter must go somewhere else. To help de-clutter, put large items in a box and store them in the hall closet or under the bed, and stack loose papers in tall baskets, preferably with lids, that can double as hiding spaces and decor.

By simply straightening up the room, you'll be less burdened without the reminders of looming projects and feel more relaxed.

2. Don't use your bedroom as storage. This is similar to the previous suggestion, except this is a more permanent problem. As much as possible, remove stored items from your room. This requires an investment of time. Take a day to sort through the stored items and decide which need to be put away in their proper place

Then take advantage of hidden spaces in your house to store the leftover items, such as:

- *Space under beds.* Invest in storage boxes that are made to fit under the bed and roll for easy access. If you are storing toys and children's clothing, utilize this space in children's rooms, as well.
- *Trunks.* Depending on the size, trunks can double as tables and/or decorations in a bedroom or living area. It gives both an aesthetic value and a practical one.
- *Baskets.* This is another valuable de-cluttering item. You can fill baskets with storage and put them on a bookshelf or under tables as decorations.

3. Choose colors that soothe. The color scheme you choose is as important as the decorations. The reason is that colors have a way of connecting with emotions.

Sharon Hanby-Robie and Deb Strubel, authors of *Beautiful Places, Spiritual Spaces* write, "Decorate your home with the colors you and your family love. It doesn't matter what the latest trends are or what the fashion gurus think. What *does* matter is that you love your home and that your choices make sense for you and your family."

If you don't know what colors and styles you like, start looking through home magazines and catalogs. Tear out pages that have colors and designs you are drawn to. Soon, you will begin to see a pattern develop, and you can use these ideas to decorate your own bedroom.

4. Use many of your best decorations. Women often use their best décor for the living room, den, or kitchen, where guests are most likely to frequent, and send the leftovers to the bedroom.

But the heart of your home lies within the relationship between husband and wife, so the bedroom should be a priority. Not only that, but your spouse will appreciate the extra attention to enhance your romance.

Go through your house and find several of your best decorations that fit with the color scheme in your bedroom. Then find a place for them, being careful not to create more clutter, but instead flatter the room. Put as much effort into this room as you would a room with higher traffic.

5. Use decorations to remind you of special memories. Frame and display photos from your wedding and honeymoon, or from other special times together. Maybe frame a copy of your wedding vows. They will remind you of how your love blossoms and grows over the years.

6. Invest in candles and burn them often. Some couples use candles mainly to decorate tables and shelves. But they miss out on the soft lighting and subtle fragrances that candles can offer a room. Nothing gives a romantic ambiance like candlelight, so find several fragrances and colors you and your spouse love, and make it a habit of burning them.

7. Spray linens and clothing with refreshing scents. Linen spray is a quick and easy way to keep sheets smelling fresh, and the soothing fragrances can calm a stressed loved one. In the same way, body sprays can also keep *you* smelling fresh and even sweeten your time together.

8. Take out the screens. Spending time staring at screens keeps the attention off your lives and onto shadows of life. Before you know it, your time together before bed slips away through the world of media.

Bob DeMoss, author of *T.V.: The Great Escape*, wrote, "I am convinced that the simple decision to unplug [screens even] for just one month has the power to revolutionize our relationships with our spouse, our children, our world, and most importantly with our God." Just by the simple act of removing screens, you open free time to reconnect with your spouse in a special way without distractions.

9. Play romantic music. There is something in music that can make or break the mood in a room. Whether you use a full stereo set with surround sound, or simple speakers, find a way to play music in your bedroom.

Choose a variety of music that soothes both you and your spouse, whether it's a collection of jazz, classical, or vintage rock, and don't forget to include songs that carry special meanings and memories. Make it a habit of putting on your favorite tunes to both relax and create a loving mood.

10. Wear an attitude to match. A beautiful bedroom only provides half the romance. If you give your spouse the cold shoulder, or use the bedroom to manipulate to get what you want, it will not be the warm place of love that it was meant to be.

Work to make your time in the bedroom a time of building up your marriage emotionally and spiritually.

Pray together regularly, avoid getting into conflicts before bedtime, and make efforts to communicate in loving ways.

If you practice these things, no matter how your bedroom looks to the eye, the heart will recognize it as a place of true love.

Discover more content by Sabrina McDonald at sabrinamcdonald.com, where you can read articles, listen to podcasts, and subscribe to her email newsletter.
You can also contact Sabrina for speaking, writing, and questions regarding more information about raising spiritually strong kids.

Check out more books by Sabrina McDonald:

A Home Built from Love and Loss: Coming Together as a Blended Family

The Blessings of Loneliness

Write God in Deeper: Journal Your Way to a Richer Faith

Made in the USA
Columbia, SC
05 February 2025